NATIONAL GEOGRAPHIC KiDS

MYTHS

BUSTED! 3

JUST WHEN YOU THOUGHT YOU KNEW WHAT YOU KNEW . . .

Emily Krieger

Illustrations by Tom Nick Cocotos

NATIONAL GEOGRAPHIC

WASHINGTON, D.C.

WORLD'S FASTEST ANIMAL

CONTENTS

MYTH

YOU'D EXPLODE IF YOU TRIED TO  FLOAT IN SPACE WITHOUT WEARING A SUIT.

ORIGIN

Let's start this book off with a bang! But one that explodes a myth, not a person. This misunderstanding likely stems from the pressurized space suits astronauts wear. These suits protect wearers from space's extremely low air pressure by creating comfortable air pressure inside. We know from high-altitude flights that bodies exposed to very low or no air pressure begin to swell (among other things).

THE GOOD NEWS: People with a leaky space suit or no space suit at all wouldn't swell and swell and swell until they exploded in space. Basically, their skin would hold them in. The bad news: They would pass out from lack of oxygen within seconds and die within minutes. And over time, their body would freeze or get a nasty sunburn.

A space suit weighs approximately 280 pounds (127 kg) on the ground, but in space, IT WEIGHS NOTHING.

9

WARM MILK MAKES YOU SLEEPY.

ORIGIN

Some people swear by warm milk as a sleep aid. They often credit the temperature of the beverage and a chemical it contains called tryptophan, which is also found in turkey, tofu, pumpkin seeds, peanuts, and other foods.

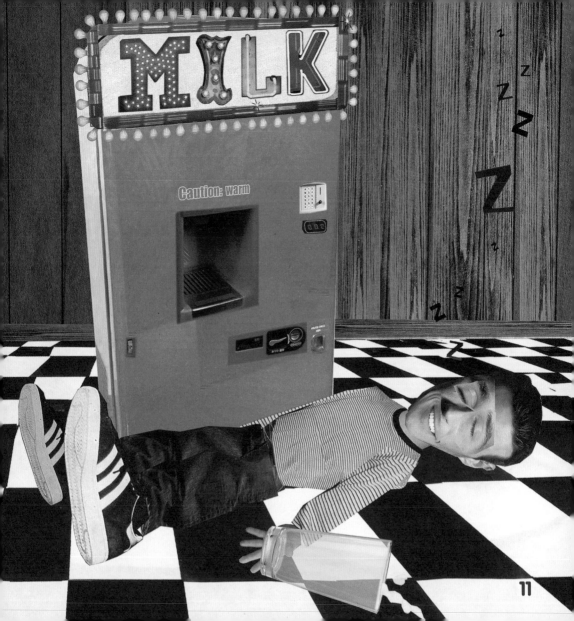

BUSTED!

WARM MILK MAY WORK AS A SLEEP AID FOR SOME PEOPLE,

but evidence shows it's not likely for the reasons they think. Sleep researchers recommend having good sleep hygiene, or a few things you do every night to help transition yourself to bedtime. For example, they recommend turning off TVs, computers, and phones; dimming lights; and avoiding big meals right before bed. Drinking warm milk as part of a pre-bedtime routine can act as a reminder to the mind and body that it's time to wind down.

"MILK TOOTH" is another name for a baby tooth.

MYTH

JULIUS CAESAR INVENTED THE CAESAR SALAD.

ORIGIN

The ancient Roman ruler is one of the most famous historical figures of all time—and certainly the most well-known Caesar. Therefore, many people assume he must be responsible for the salad that bears his name.

BUSTED!

Ancient Roman recipes more than 2,000 years old include instructions for how to prepare FLAMINGO, OSTRICH, AND PEACOCK.

YOU CAN CREDIT JULIUS CAESAR WITH A LOT OF THINGS—BUT NOT THE CAESAR SALAD. Instead, credit is usually given to Caesar Cardini, who is said to have created the salad after customers swarmed his Tijuana, Mexico, restaurant one night in 1924. Afraid he would run out of fresh vegetables to serve, Cardini concocted a salad from romaine lettuce, eggs, and several other ingredients on hand.

MYTH

CHEETAHS ARE THE FASTEST ANIMALS IN THE WORLD.

ORIGIN

At 70 miles an hour (112.7 km/h), cheetahs are the fastest animals *on land*, but are they truly the fastest on Earth?

BUSTED!

NOT SO FAST!

Peregrine falcons can reach speeds of more than 200 miles an hour (321.9 km/h) *in the air*. At sea, sailfish give cheetahs a run—or rather, swim—for their money at 68 miles an hour (109.4 km/h).

Despite weighing up to 345 pounds (156.5 kg), North African OSTRICHES can run as fast as 45 miles an hour (72.4 km/h)!

MORE RECORD-BREAKING ANIMALS

LONGEST ANIMAL
BOOTLACE WORM
>> 180 feet (55 m)

LONGEST FUR ON A CAT
COLONEL MEOW
<< 9 inches (22.87 cm)

STRONGEST ANIMAL
RHINOCEROS BEETLE
>> can lift 850 times its own weight

ANIMAL PHOTOGRAPHED WITH THE MOST CELEBRITIES
THE DOG LUCKY DIAMOND
<< 363 celebs

MOST LEGS
MILLIPEDE
>> 750

MYTH

HUMANS EVOLVED FROM CHIMPANZEES.

ORIGIN

The two types of animals are both primates and are often called cousins. We also share about 99 percent of our DNA, or genetic material. And you may have seen illustrations of how humans evolved, or changed slowly over a long period of time, from earlier species that looked kind of like chimps. Even today, humans and chimps look and act very similarly.

SMITH FAMILY REUNION

23

BUSTED!

HUMANS DIDN'T EVOLVE FROM CHIMPS.

And chimps didn't evolve from humans. Rather, chimps and humans evolved separately, alongside each other, from a distant, shared relative. Among all the species in the world, we are each other's closest living relative. Briana Pobiner, a scientist who studies human evolution at the Smithsonian Institution in Washington, D.C., compares human and chimp evolution to two branches of a tree. Although the branches are now separate from each other, they both came from a single, larger branch or trunk. Similarly, humans and chimps are now separate, but both evolved from the same, now extinct species about six million to eight million years ago.

As recently as about 70,000 YEARS AGO, there were several species of humans living on Earth at the same time. Only one of those survives today— our species, *HOMO SAPIENS*.

MYTH

BOYS ARE NATURALLY BETTER AT MATH THAN GIRLS ARE.

ORIGIN

People who say boys really are better at math point to tests that boys have performed better on. But the idea has been around a long time—before those tests, and even before girls began attending school as regularly as boys.

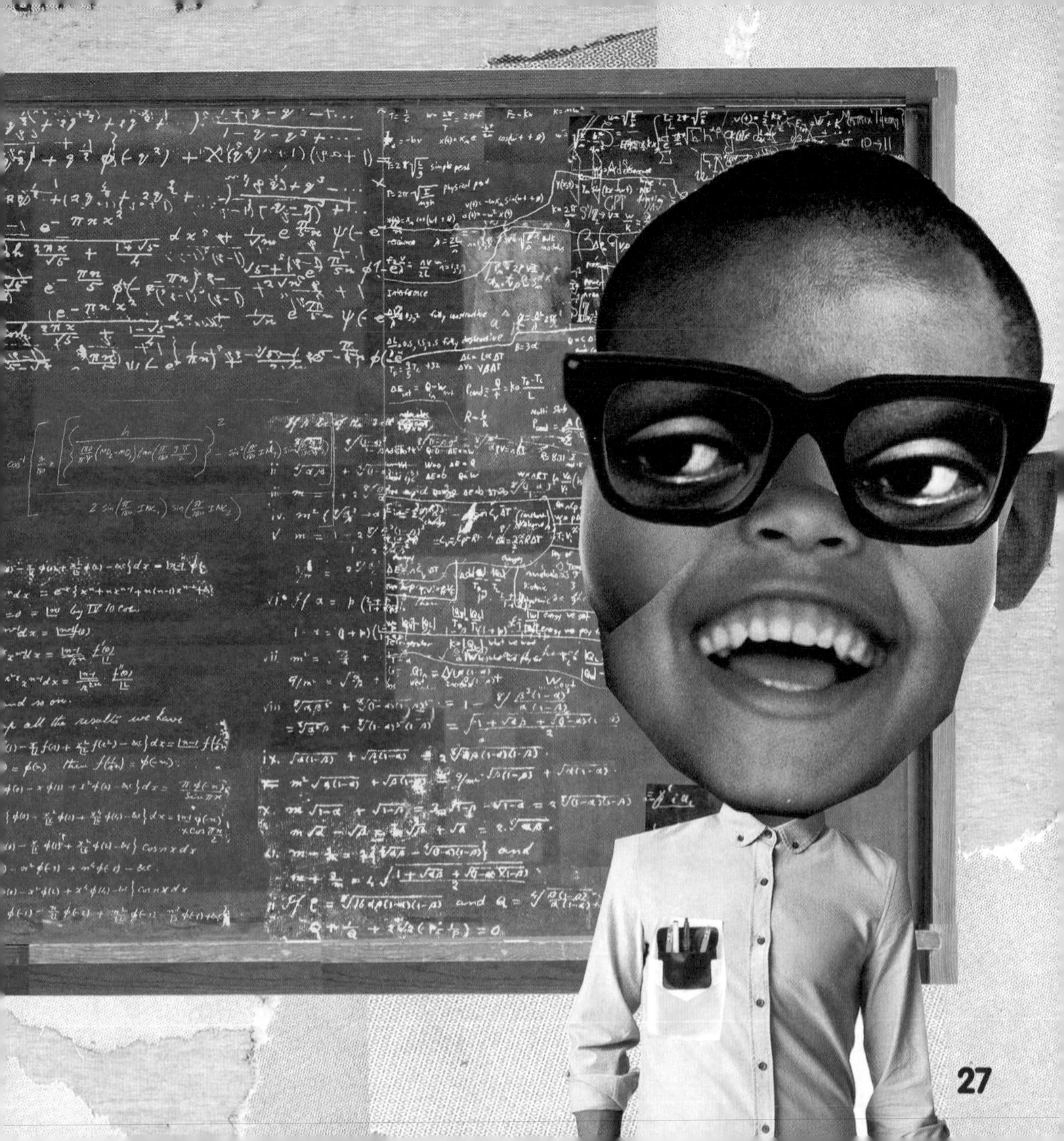

BUSTED!

MANY SCIENTISTS HAVE STUDIED WHETHER BOYS ARE BETTER AT MATH THAN GIRLS, AND IF SO, WHY.

Some of the biggest studies have looked at the math knowledge and skills of students in dozens of countries. They've found that in some countries, boys do perform better than girls on math tests. In other countries, however, girls outperform boys. In still other countries, boys and girls perform equally. So what do these findings mean? They suggest there's no evidence that boys are born with a better ability to perform math than girls are. Scientists say that in countries where boys beat girls at math, it's likely because of differences in the way boys and girls are treated within their culture. For example, boys may be encouraged to explore an interest in math more than girls are. And boys may be encouraged to feel more confident about their math abilities than girls are. Yet another explanation: Boys may perform better on a single, competitive test—like a math exam—than girls do. The good news is we can work to change these differences. So the next time someone says that boys are just "naturally" better at math than girls, tell them the evidence for this just doesn't add up.

A 2013 study found that children with a BIGGER HIPPOCAMPUS—a part of the brain—improved the most in math after being tutored in the subject for eight weeks.

MYTH

LEMMINGS INTENTIONALLY JUMP OFF CLIFFS TOGETHER.

ORIGIN

Lemmings are furry little rodents whose populations can rise and fall dramatically. For centuries, people have come up with explanations for why the number of lemmings in a place can change so much in a short period of time. One explanation: When a population of lemmings grows too large, the rodents will run off cliffs together into the water to drown themselves.

CANNONBALL

In the popular 1990s video game *Lemmings,* players had to maneuver HUMANLIKE LEMMINGS through a series of obstacles, including avoiding falling into water.

LEMMINGS DON'T TRY TO DROWN THEMSELVES.

The myth has its roots in some truth, though. Sometimes a group of lemmings will run away to find a new home with more food. In their search, they may come upon a cliff or shoreline and pile up at its edge. In the push and shove, lemmings may accidentally get bumped into the water. Some also leap in and try to swim across. But lemmings don't make a habit of marching to cliffs and throwing themselves off to keep their numbers down. Rather, scientists point to factors such as a decrease in food and an increase in predators as causes for lemming population declines.

MYTH

A DOG IS SICK IF ITS NOSE IS DRY AND WARM.

ORIGIN

A dog's nose is often—but not always—wet and cool. So it may seem like something is off if it's dry and warm.

A DRY, WARM NOSE

does not automatically mean your pooch is sick. So don't panic. Instead, take your dog's temperature, watch to make sure it's eating and drinking regularly, and look for signs of discomfort, such as limping or a reluctance to move, or changes in its bathroom habits. These are more reliable ways to tell if your dog is feeling well.

A HEALTHY DOG'S TEMPERATURE is typically between 101 and 102.5°F (38.3 to 39.2°C); A HEALTHY HUMAN'S is slightly cooler, averaging 98.6°F (37°C).

MYTH

TORNADOES OCCUR ONLY IN FLAT PLACES.

ORIGIN

People typically think of tornadoes as wreaking havoc in flat, midwestern U.S. landscapes (like the twister that totaled Dorothy's Kansas home in *The Wizard of Oz*). And it's true that in the United States, flatter states typically experience more tornadoes.

BUSTED!

MOUNTAINS DON'T MAKE PEOPLE SAFE FROM TORNADOES.

In fact, in the United States, two twisters have been seen at elevations exceeding 11,500 feet (3,505 m). In 2004, a hiker photographed a tornado in California's Sierra Nevada range. In 2012, a Colorado man snapped a photo of a twister touching down on Mount Evans, west of Denver. As a rule of thumb, places between 30° and 50° north or south latitude are more prone to tornadoes. The United States, which sits smack-dab between 30° and 50° north latitude, currently leads the world in most tornadoes: usually more than 1,000 twisters each year.

Canada, the country that comes in second place for most tornadoes, has only ABOUT 100 PER YEAR. That's ten times fewer than the first-place holder, the United States!

MORE TORNADO MYTHS BUSTED

TORNADOES ARE MORE LIKELY TO STRIKE MOBILE HOME PARKS. Mobile homes don't "attract" tornadoes. It may seem that way since the easily damaged structures often end up on the news.

TORNADOES "SKIP" ALONG THEIR PATHS. Twisters don't alternate between touching down and lifting off. Differences in damage among homes in a tornado's path are instead due to factors such as how they were built.

TRAILER

PARK

CORNER

40

TORNADOES DON'T HIT BIG CITIES. Twisters have touched down in large U.S. cities, including Dallas, St. Louis, Miami, and Salt Lake City.

RIVERS PROTECT PEOPLE FROM TORNADOES. Twisters can travel across and even along rivers.

TORNADOES NEVER STRIKE THE SAME PLACE TWICE. Tornadoes, like lightning, can, in fact, strike the same place twice.

MYTH

DIAMONDS COME FROM COAL.

ORIGIN

The *Superman* comics helped popularize this myth: The superhero creates a diamond simply by squeezing coal in his bare hand.

IT IS POSSIBLE TO PRODUCE DIAMONDS FROM COAL IN A LAB.

But diamonds that are mined for sale and worn as jewelry don't come from coal. These gems are even older than coal and formed deeper in the earth than coal. We have access to them today because long ago, violent volcanic eruptions brought the gems closer to Earth's surface. Diamonds and coal do have some things in common, though: Both are made of carbon. And to form, both require high temperatures and lots of pressure (much higher temperatures and lots more pressure for diamonds). But these forces come from within Earth, not in a superhero's fist.

METEORITES contain teeny-tiny diamonds.

MYTH

THE MORE YOU SWEAT, THE HARDER YOU'RE WORKING.

ORIGIN

A good workout often works up a good sweat. So, many people figure more sweat means a better workout.

SWEAT BEES are attracted to the perspiration on people's skin.

BUSTED!

YOU CAN'T COUNT ON SWEAT to tell you how hard you're working or how many calories you're burning. To understand why this is, you have to first understand why you sweat: to cool off. When calories are burned, heat is released into the body. The body needs to shed that heat to keep a comfortable temperature, around 98.6°F (37°C). So the body produces sweat, which whisks away the heat when it evaporates, or turns from a liquid into a gas. How quickly sweat evaporates, taking that heat with it, and how quickly the body is cooled depends on several factors. These include the weather; a person's fitness level, clothing, and size; how hydrated they are; even whether they're male or female, says Anthony Wall, director of professional education at the American Council on Exercise. These factors vary from person to person and even from day to day. So there is no formula for using sweat to calculate calories burned. The body will sweat as long as it needs to cool off and has enough water to produce perspiration.

MYTH

PEOPLE THOUGHT THE

WORLD WAS FLAT

UNTIL CHRISTOPHER

COLUMBUS SAILED ACROSS THE ATLANTIC OCEAN IN 1492.

ORIGIN

This idea is an exaggeration of what people in Columbus's time thought. Some did indeed find it hard to believe that the world was round and not flat. However, others—most notably many scientists and mathematicians and other educated people—believed Earth was shaped like a sphere.

BUSTED!

GREEK PHILOSOPHERS DEBATED AND WROTE ABOUT A SPHERICAL EARTH

nearly 2,000 years before Columbus's famous voyage. So he didn't blow everyone's minds when his ships failed to sail right over the edge of a flat Earth. The bigger unknown was whether Columbus's calculations for the voyage were correct. In fact, he vastly underestimated the size of Earth, and thus the size of the ocean he set out to cross.

In Hawaii, people celebrate Discoverers' Day—in honor of the discovery of the islands—on COLUMBUS DAY, the second Monday in October.

49

MYTH

COMPETING IN GYMNASTICS STUNTS YOUR GROWTH.

ORIGIN

Sure, a lot of gymnasts are on the shorter side. But are they short because of gymnastics?

BUSTED!

THE INTERNATIONAL GYMNASTICS FEDERATION

asked scientists to investigate this claim after years of debate over it. The 2013 study found no evidence that the sport stunts growth. A previous study of gymnasts, published in 2000, also failed to turn up any evidence that gymnastics stunts growth. Instead, experts say, shorter people dominate the sport likely because they have a lower center of gravity, which increases their stability.

When gymnastics made its debut at the 1896 Athens, Greece, Olympics, the sport included ROCK-LIFTING AND CLUB-SWINGING EVENTS.

MYTH

YOU CAN TELL A LADYBUG'S AGE BY COUNTING ITS SPOTS.

ORIGIN

Ladybugs—cute little winged beetles—have many myths surrounding them. Most are positive, such as they bring good luck or a good harvest. Counting a ladybug's spots to tell its age may stem from the fact that you can count a tree's rings to tell how old it is.

BUSTED!

Ladybugs are also called LADYBIRDS in Great Britain, Canada, and Australia.

YOU CAN'T COUNT ON SPOTS TO TELL A LADYBUG'S AGE.

For starters, not all ladybugs have spots. Some are striped, checkered, or have no pattern at all. There are actually more than 5,000 different species, or types, of ladybugs in the world, with many different appearances. And adults don't change their spots, anyway, gaining one on each birthday, for example. If they did, most ladybugs would have only one or two spots, since the insects seldom live longer than two years.

MYTH

BREATHING REQUIRES  LUNGS.

ORIGIN

All animals draw in oxygen and emit carbon dioxide. Many—humans, even marine mammals—do this with lungs. But do all creatures breathe in this way?

FISH ANATOMY

mandible
pre-maxillary
maxillary
nostrils
Gill Filament
branchiostegal rays
dorsal spines
preopercle
lungs
subopercle
pelvic fins
dorsal fin
caudal fin

BUSTED!

Humans have two lungs, but they DON'T LOOK EXACTLY THE SAME. The left one is slightly smaller, to make room for the heart. It's also made up of two lobes, while the right lung is made up of three.

NOT ALL ANIMALS RELY ON LUNGS TO GET OXYGEN AND GET RID OF CARBON DIOXIDE.

Fish and tiny tadpoles, or young amphibians, use gills to breathe. Some adult amphibians rely on gills, but most breathe through their lungs, moist skin, and the lining of their mouth. A few breathe only through their skin and mouth. Worms, lacking lungs, breathe through their damp skin. Other animals, such as insects, acquire oxygen through tiny holes called spiracles and distribute it throughout the body via a network of tubes. There's even a mammal—a mouselike marsupial called a Julia Creek dunnart—that breathes through its skin as a newborn.

MYTH

WALKING UNDER  A LADDER BRINGS BAD LUCK.

ORIGIN

In part, this myth probably has its origins in plain old common sense: It's safer to *not* walk beneath someone or something that's precariously perched (and might have things like paint dripping from it).

THIS MYTH IS AN EXAMPLE OF A SUPERSTITION, which is an

idea or behavior not based on facts. That means there's no proof that walking beneath a ladder brings bad luck or somehow causes bad things to start happening to you afterward. So, if you're in a pinch and can't walk around a ladder, don't worry. But do be careful as you pass beneath it—and while atop one. The Ladder Association, based in the United Kingdom, suggests spending no more than 30 minutes at a time on a ladder, for safety.

BUSTED!

In 2011, a Guinean man took 75 steps BACKWARD ON A LADDER while at the same time controlling a soccer ball with his feet.

MYTH

THERE IS A VAMPIRE CALLED
COUNT DRACULA
THAT LIVES IN TRANSYLVANIA.

ORIGIN

In the 1400s, there was a real-life, fearsome ruler who went by the name Dracula.
He was born in Transylvania, a region in what is now the country of Romania. In 1897,
Bram Stoker published his book *Dracula*. It was about a creepy, bloodsucking count who
resided in a castle in Transylvania.

Welcome
TO
TRANSYLVANIA

BUSTED!

THE REAL DRACULA is the one widely known as a bloodthirsty ruler, not a bloodsucker. Vampires, including Stoker's Count Dracula, are made-up monsters. The real-life Dracula didn't suck people's blood and have to head indoors at dawn. He was, however, still a pretty spooky guy: He was known for skewering people on stakes to scare others. Further mixing fact with fiction is Bran Castle, in Transylvania. It's said to be the real-life inspiration for the fake Dracula's castle.

People used to believe that you could keep a vampire busy—meaning, off your neck—by offering it lots of TINY THINGS TO COUNT, such as a handful of rice. Supposedly the monster wouldn't be able to resist.

MYTH

CINCO
DE MAYO IS
MEXICAN
INDEPENDENCE DAY.

ORIGIN

Cinco de Mayo, Spanish for "fifth of May," has been celebrated in America and—to a far lesser extent—in Mexico on its namesake day since the mid-1800s. But many people today don't know the history behind the holiday. So they assume two things: It's Mexico's Independence Day and it's a big celebration in both countries.

The first celebration of the United States' independence from Great Britain was held on JULY 8, NOT JULY 4, 1776, in Philadelphia.

BUSTED!

MEXICO'S INDEPENDENCE DAY IS ACTUALLY SEPTEMBER 16.

Cinco de Mayo commemorates the day that Mexicans stopped the French army from invading the city of Puebla—May 5, 1862. The holiday has been part of U.S. culture since word of the Mexican victory first reached Latinos living in the American West. In fact, "Cinco de Mayo is not, in its origins, a Mexican holiday at all but rather an American one, created by Latinos in California in the middle of the nineteenth century," wrote University of California, Los Angeles, professor David Hayes-Bautista in his book *El Cinco de Mayo: An American Tradition*. Today, the holiday is celebrated far more in America than in Mexico, where Mexican Independence Day is a much bigger deal.

MORE
INDEPENDENCE
DAYS
FROM AROUND
THE WORLD

OCT 1 1978 TUVALU

NOV 30 1966 BARBADOS

MAR 21 1990 NAMIBIA

SEPT 21 1981 BELIZE

JULY 11 1921 MONGOLIA

IRELAND

DEC
6
1921

NEW ZEALAND

SEPT
26
1907

FINLAND

DEC
6
1917

PERU

JULY
28
1821

JUNE
26
1960

MADAGASCAR
Madagascar's citizens celebrate their country's independence day with a laser light show, parade, concert, and fireworks.

AFGHANISTAN

AUG
19
1919

RABBITS CAN'T PASS GAS THROUGH THEIR REAR.

ORIGIN

It's true that rabbits can't burp. But does that mean they also can't pass gas from their rear?

RABBITS CAN TOTALLY TOOT,

says Seattle veterinarian Dan Lejnieks. "They do so all the time, sometimes audibly." He should know: He sees rabbits regularly at his practice and has heard them toot in his exam rooms. The animals do sometimes develop a dangerous condition called gastric stasis that makes it difficult for them to toot, he notes. He gives these gassy patients medicine to get things moving. Other treatments include belly rubs, warmth, and offering herbs like cilantro, basil, and fennel.

> **DARIUS THE RABBIT** weighed in at 49 pounds (22 kg) to claim the title of world's biggest bunny.

79

MYTH

RACCOONS WASH THEIR FOOD BEFORE EVERY MEAL.

ORIGIN

Raccoons often forage for food along shorelines, dabbing their paws in the water in search of a tasty morsel. Sometimes, after catching something to eat, they'll make a motion with it in the water that resembles washing. And captive raccoons have been observed dousing food in water when it's nearby. Are these animals doing this because they're neat freaks? And do they have to wash their food before every meal?

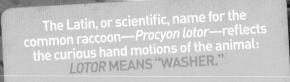

WAITER, THERE'S A FLY IN MY GARBAGE.

The Latin, or scientific, name for the common raccoon—*Procyon lotor*—reflects the curious hand motions of the animal: *LOTOR* MEANS "WASHER."

BUSTED!

THE IDEA THAT RACCOONS make such motions to clean their food is a "natural guess," says Weber State University zoologist Sam Zeveloff, author of *Raccoons: A Natural History*. But studies of raccoon hands suggest something else, he says. Scientists have found that raccoon hands are very sensitive, more like our hands or a chimpanzee's than like a dog's or cat's paws. "Their hands do appear to be more sensitive when they're wet and made softer," says Zeveloff. So, he concludes, "what I think is a more compelling idea is that because their hands and fingertips are so sensitive, they may actually just be manipulating or feeling an item in water to increase the sensitivity of their touch." But even so, raccoons don't always wet their food—far from it, in fact. "They are increasingly found in more arid and urban areas," Zeveloff points out, and will readily eat food even without water.

MORE RACCOON MYTHS BUSTED

ALL RACCOONS HAVE RABIES. Not all raccoons have rabies, and they aren't the only animals that can carry the disease. Skunks, bats, and foxes can too.

Coati

RACCOONS ARE MOST CLOSELY RELATED TO OR ACTUALLY ARE A TYPE OF RODENT, FOX, OR BEAR. Raccoons are in the same family as creatures called coatis, kinkajous, and olingos.

RACCOONS ARE STRICTLY NOCTURNAL. These highly adaptable animals can be active during the daytime too.

Fox

RACCOONS DON'T HAVE SALIVARY GLANDS. This disproven belief used to be the explanation for why raccoons "wash" their food.

STORING BATTERIES IN THE REFRIGERATOR OR FREEZER MAKES THEM LAST LONGER.

ORIGIN

You never want to let a battery get hot or wet. And keeping a battery cold slows its self-discharge rate, or how quickly it loses energy while not in use.

BUSTED!

YOU DON'T NEED TO PUT BATTERIES IN COLD STORAGE.

In fact, major battery manufacturers say it's not recommended or necessary. They instead advise storing batteries at room temperature and away from moisture—which a fridge and freezer are full of. If you really wanted to chill your batteries, however, those "with the fastest self-discharge are those that you would refrigerate," says Curtis Randolph, CEO of the Responsible Energy Corporation. A type of battery called nickel-metal hydride loses energy fastest when not in use, he says. However, he notes, "cold will prevent power being drawn." So refrigerated or frozen batteries will need to warm up before being put to use. "I don't find that convenient," says Randolph, so instead, "I put my rechargeable batteries in a smart charger."

You can build
a battery with
a POTATO.

89

MYTH

SPF 30
IS TWICE THE
PROTECTION OF
SPF 15.

ORIGIN

All sunscreens carry a sun protection factor, or SPF, to let users know how much protection they're receiving from the sun's rays. Fifteen multiplied by 2 is 30, so it would make sense that a sunscreen with SPF 30 would be twice as strong as one with SPF 15.

BUSTED!

SUNSCREEN RATINGS DON'T FOLLOW SIMPLE MATH.

What SPF means exactly is more complex. The U.S. Environmental Protection Agency explains that SPF 15 sunscreens protect against 93 percent of UVB rays. SPF 30 protects against 97 percent of UVB rays. Using an SPF of 30 or higher is generally recommended. And experts advise using sunscreens that are "broad-spectrum," which means they also protect against UVA rays, which have longer wavelengths than UVB rays. And no sunscreen sticks around forever, so make sure to reapply often.

People have gotten a sunburn on the ROOF OF THEIR MOUTH while climbing Mount Everest. Sunlight reflecting off of ice and snow hits the inside of panting climbers' mouths.

MYTH

MARY SHELLEY'S 1818 BOOK, *FRANKENSTEIN*, IS NAMED FOR ITS MAN-MADE MONSTER.

ORIGIN

Shelley's book told the creepy tale of a man who created a monster—one without a name. Today, people most often refer to that monster as Frankenstein.

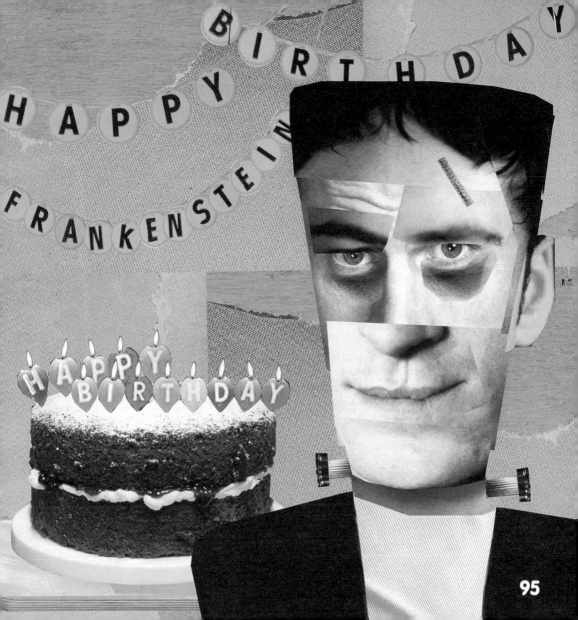

HAPPY BIRTHDAY FRANKENSTEIN

HAPPY BIRTHDAY

95

The POPULAR PHRASE "It's alive!" is often associated with the moment Frankenstein's monster comes to life. But the phrase NEVER APPEARS in the book. Instead, it comes from a famous scene in the 1931 movie *Frankenstein*.

IN THE BOOK, THAT MAN—NOT THE MONSTER—WAS NAMED FRANKENSTEIN.

Victor Frankenstein, to be exact. The creature we think of today as having a big green, square-shaped head and neck bolts is not Frankenstein, but rather Frankenstein's monster. (And by the way, Shelley did not describe the monster as a green blockhead with neck bolts; that depiction was popularized years later.) Some people argue that because Frankenstein created the creature, he was its father, and therefore the creature should have his last name. In reality, though, Shelley never gave the monster a name. Instead, throughout the book, Frankenstein refers to his monster as "devil."

97

MYTH

PEOPLE MUST DRINK
EIGHT GLASSES
OF WATER A DAY TO STAY HYDRATED.

I HOPE THERE IS A BATHROOM AROUND HERE!

ORIGIN

More than half of the human body is water. So it's important to stay properly hydrated. But how much water is enough? The root of the eight-glasses-a-day recommendation is often traced to dietary guidelines published in 1945 by the U.S. Food and Nutrition Board. Those guidelines called for the average male to ingest 2,500 milliliters (84 oz) of fluid a day; 1 milliliter of water for every kilocalorie consumed. Over time, drinking 64 ounces—or eight 8-ounce glasses—of water a day became the rule of thumb.

BUSTED!

THERE IS NO EVIDENCE THAT GULPING DOWN EIGHT GLASSES of water a day is a one-size-fits-all formula. Some doctors and scientists advise more, some less. In 2005, the U.S. National Research Council recommended kids ages 9 to 13 ingest 2,400 milliliters (81 oz) of water a day. That figure, though, includes water from food (think about biting into a juicy piece of fruit) and beverages other than water. Keep in mind, too, that factors such as hot temperatures and strenuous exercise will alter how much water a person ideally needs.

GALÁPAGOS TORTOISES can go a year without drinking (or eating).

MYTH

GARLIC REPELS MOSQUITOES.

ORIGIN
Garlic's strong odor (garlic breath, anyone?) can repel people. So why not mosquitoes?

BUSTED!

UNFORTUNATELY, MOSQUITOES DON'T RESPOND TO GARLIC BREATH.
A 2005 study at the University of Connecticut Health Center gave garlic to volunteers and found no evidence that it repelled the pesky insects. It's possible that larger quantities of garlic consumed over longer periods of time might work. But there's no evidence for this. And even if there were, people eating this much garlic would probably repel more than mosquitoes.

Only FEMALE mosquitoes feed on blood.

MYTH

WAKING A SLEEPWALKING PERSON COULD KILL THEM.

ORIGIN

It can be dangerous to wake a sleepwalker—but more for you, not them. That's because sleepwalkers upon waking are often confused and may react violently in fear.

BUSTED!

SLEEPWALKERS CAN'T BE KILLED BY SOMEONE SIMPLY WAKING THEM UP.

But they could harm themselves while sleepwalking, by falling down stairs or picking up sharp objects—they sometimes even cook food and drive cars! So don't ignore sleepwalkers. Instead, try to gently guide them back to bed. If they resist and you must wake them, don't shake them; use sounds. Once awake, expect them to be disoriented, perhaps frightened, and to have no memory of what they did while sleepwalking.

In 2005, a 15-year-old London girl had to be rescued from atop a 130-FOOT (39.6-M) CRANE after climbing it while sleepwalking!

TO GET RID OF WARTS, RUB PENNIES ON THEM.

ORIGIN

This myth likely sprang from a place of desperation; no one likes warts. So over time, people have invented a lot of wacky ways to supposedly get rid of them (see pp. 108–109).

BUSTED!

YOU'RE BETTER OFF SAVING YOUR PENNIES

for a rainy day, because they won't work on warts. And, if you're curious, neither do dimes, nickels, or quarters—or any currency. You should instead find someone who can use science, not superstition, to help you. A doctor can remove warts in several ways, such as by treating them with creams or "paints," by zapping them with lasers, or by freezing them with liquid nitrogen.

The real-life type of warts depicted on WITCHES' NOSES and chins are called filiform warts.

MORE SILLY MYTHS

ABOUT HOW TO GET RID OF

WARTS

STICK A SLUG ON TOP OF A WART.

SPLIT A PEA, RUB EACH HALF OVER THE WART WHILE WISHING IT UPON SOMEONE ELSE, THEN THROW ONE HALF OVER YOUR SHOULDER AND THE OTHER INTO A RIVER.

SPIT ON A WART.

109

MYTH

TWINKIES NEVER GO BAD.

ORIGIN

There's a rumor that the sweet treats never expire because they're made of only artificial ingredients.

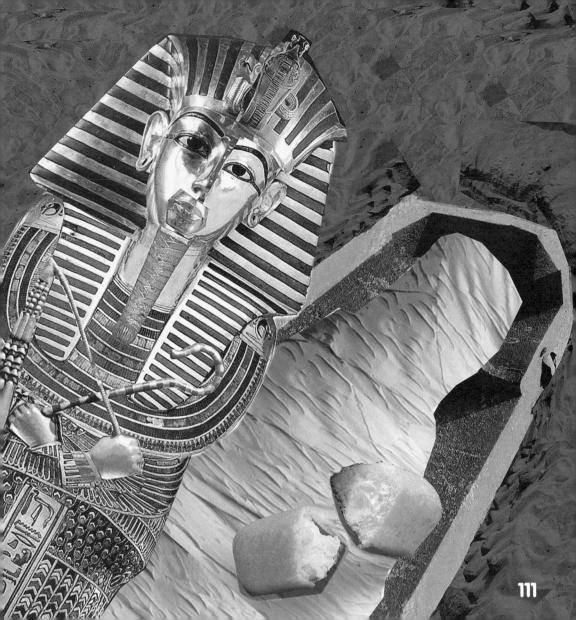

BUSTED!

TWINKIES ARE MOSTLY FLOUR AND SUGAR.

And they don't last forever. In fact, they don't last very long at all. In 2012, their shelf life was extended from 26 days to 45 days. If they did last forever, and just a small fraction went uneaten, there would be a lot of Twinkies lying around for eternity: Half a billion are made each year!

In 1995, TWO STUDENTS AT RICE UNIVERSITY in Houston, Texas, U.S.A., conducted a series of silly experiments during finals week "to determine the properties of that incredible food, the Twinkie." They pureed Twinkies in a blender, dropped them from a sixth-floor window, lit them on fire, and even tested the treats for SIGNS OF INTELLIGENCE.

MYTH

THERE'S A DARK SIDE OF THE MOON.

ORIGIN

The "dark side of the moon" is the nickname for the side of the moon we never see from Earth. But does that side never see the sun?

BUSTED!

THERE IS A SIDE OF EARTH'S SATELLITE THAT WE NEVER SEE,

but that doesn't mean that side never sees the sun. All sides of the moon see the sun. In fact, the "dark side" of the moon directly faces the sun and is lit up by it during what we call a "new moon" phase here on Earth. During this phase, we see the side of the moon that isn't being lit up by the sun. So there really is no permanently dark side of the moon. Astronomers instead sometimes refer to the side of the moon that always faces away from Earth as the "far side." Spacecraft snapped the first photos of it in 1959, the first video in 2012.

Other planets have moons, but they're given names, such as IO, EUROPA, SKOLL, and even MARGARET. Earth's moon is simply named "the moon."

MORE MOON MYTHS BUSTED

THE MOON ITSELF PRODUCES LIGHT, JUST LIKE THE SUN. The moon, just like the planets, shines because of reflected sunlight.

THE MOON IS PERFECTLY ROUND. It's not; it's lopsided.

THE MOON IS MADE OF CHEESE. Unfortunately, the moon is made of something far less delicious: rock and dust.

THE MOON DOESN'T ROTATE. The moon does spin. It takes 27.3 days for the moon to turn all the way around. It takes the same amount of time for the moon to orbit Earth. This helps explain why we never see the satellite's "dark side."

A "SUPERMOON" APPEARS BIGGER THAN USUAL BECAUSE THE MOON ITSELF HAS ACTUALLY GROWN IN SIZE. A supermoon appears supersize only because it's slightly closer to Earth during its orbit; the satellite itself hasn't grown larger.

MYTH

PTERODACTYLS ARE DINOSAURS.

ORIGIN

Pterodactyls resemble dinosaurs and existed at the same time as them.

DINO-DATING

BACHELOR'S NAME: Pterodactyl

BUSTED!

THIS MAY COME AS A SHOCK,

but pterodactyls—those popular, dino-like creatures that soared through the air—aren't dinosaurs. They are pterosaurs, another group of ancient reptiles. And actually, *pterodactyl* is an outdated word used to describe only one type of pterosaur.

The largest pterosaurs had A WINGSPAN OF 40 FEET (12 m)! A super-size finger—the fourth—supported each wing.

MYTH

MYTH

YOU SHOULD NEVER SLEEP IN A CLOSED ROOM WITH AN ELECTRIC FAN ON.

ORIGIN

This myth has persisted for decades in South Korea. Alerts have even been issued there for people to use fans with timers. Reasons given for these so-called fan deaths include lack of oxygen and hypothermia (dangerously low body temperature).

You wouldn't want to get close to some of the first electric fans: They had NO PROTECTIVE CAGE around their rotating blades!

BUSTED!

IT'S PERFECTLY SAFE TO SLEEP WITH A FAN ON without cracking a window or door, except in extremely hot temperatures, says climate scientist Laurence Kalkstein, at the University of Miami in Florida, U.S.A. "What's true is if it's very hot in an enclosed room and you're running a fan, what can happen is moisture is lost from the body at an increased rate and that creates a health problem," he explains. Someone in such conditions wouldn't die from lack of oxygen or hypothermia, though. "Those explanations are baloney," he says. Rather, dehydration and heat stroke would be the culprits. Indeed, the U.S. Environmental Protection Agency cautions that "using a portable electric fan alone [without air-conditioning also on in the room] when heat index temperatures exceed 99 degrees Fahrenheit actually increases the heat stress the body must respond to by blowing air that is warmer than the ideal body temperature over the skin surface." Basically, as you sweat to cool off, you would lose water. Without replenishing it, you'd eventually become dehydrated and unable to properly cool down, which would lead to a dangerous, sometimes deadly, spike in body temperature.

MYTH

MOUNT EVEREST IS THE TALLEST MOUNTAIN IN THE WORLD.

ORIGIN

Topping out at an elevation of 29,035 feet (8,850 m), Mount Everest reaches a higher elevation than any other mountain in the world.

MOUNT EVEREST REACHES THE HIGHEST HEIGHTS.

But it isn't the tallest—the distance from top to bottom—of all mountains. Hawaii's mighty Mauna Kea claims that honor, at 33,476 feet (10,203 m). But an incredible 19,678 feet (5,998 m) of the mountain sits below the sea's surface. So Mount Everest actually stands more than twice as high above the horizon as Mauna Kea.

Did you know you can ski in Hawaii?! Despite its tropical location, Mauna Kea sometimes gets enough snow for people to HIT THE SLOPES. Its name even means "white mountain."

BUSTED!

MYTH

THE SUN IS ON FIRE.

ORIGIN

When we think of something that's superhot and looks like it's on fire—such as the sun—we assume it's burning.

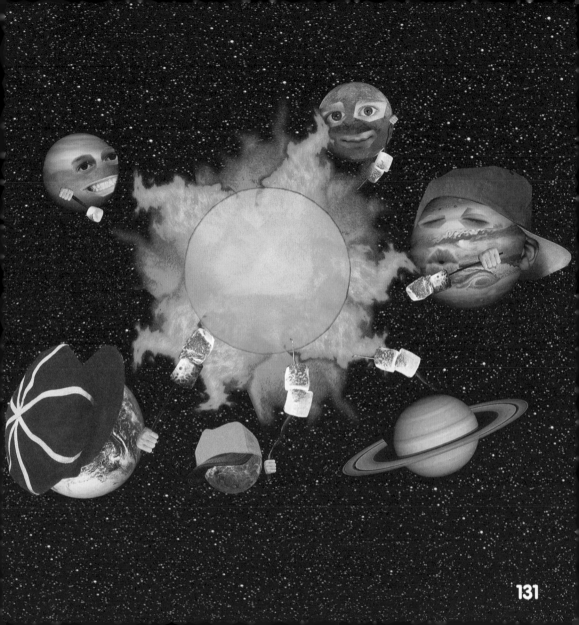

BUSTED!

UNLIKE A LOG OR A PIECE OF PAPER LIT ON FIRE, the sun is not something solid that's burning. Instead, the sun is a giant, dense ball of gas whose heat and light are powered by a process called nuclear fusion. At the sun's center, protons—teeny-tiny particles—constantly collide and fuse together. This releases a lot of energy. That energy radiates outward, creating what we see as the sun and eventually reaching us as heat and light here on Earth.

At its core, the sun is about 27 MILLION DEGREES FAHRENHEIT (15 million degrees Celsius).

MYTH

DRAGONFLIES SEW SLEEPING PEOPLE'S LIPS SHUT.

ORIGIN

This insect has been nicknamed "devil's darning needle" or "devil's needle" for more than 150 years. Its bulging eyes, long body, and big size—wingspans can stretch more than half a foot (15 cm)—remind some people of a large sewing needle buzzing about.

BUSTED!

DRAGONFLIES MAY LOOK LIKE SEWING NEEDLES,

but they can't act like one and sew your mouth shut while you're asleep. That skill would be a first for any animal. Dragonflies are still pretty amazing, though: Their four wings can move independently of one another, and they can hover in midair, stop suddenly, and even fly backward!

To distinguish dragonflies from their look-alike relatives damselflies, look at the insects' wings WHILE THEY'RE AT REST. Typically, a resting dragonfly holds its wings OUTSTRETCHED like a plane; a resting damselfly FOLDS ITS WINGS UP.

MYTH

A CURSED MUMMY ABOARD THE *TITANIC* CAUSED THE SHIP TO SINK.

ORIGIN

According to legend, an Egyptian mummy brought misfortune and death to many before it caused the *Titanic* to hit an iceberg and sink in 1912. Newspaper reports and word-of-mouth stories about the "Unlucky Mummy" varied in their details. The "Priestess of Amen-Ra," as the mummy was sometimes called—or simply her coffin lid, the story sometimes went—was reportedly aboard the ship after the British Museum in London secretly sold it to either an American or Englishman.

BUSTED!

Another item rumored to be cursed and resting on the bottom of the sea in the *Titanic* is the HOPE DIAMOND. That's a myth, too, though: The diamond is on display in the NATIONAL MUSEUM OF NATURAL HISTORY in Washington, D.C.

NO MUMMY OR COFFIN LID EVER SET SAIL ON THE *TITANIC*.

Neither appears on the list of all the items that were aboard the ship when it sank. Which makes sense because, the British Museum says, the coffin lid the legend refers to, acquired in 1889, "never left the Museum until it went to a temporary exhibition in 1990." And actually, the lid was not a lid, but a mummy board, which is placed directly on top of the mummy, not the coffin. So whom did the lid entomb at one time, and where is that mummy now? Says the museum, "The mummy to which this board belonged is said to have been left in Egypt. No inscriptions on the board identify the deceased."

MYTH

YOU'RE BORN WITH ALL THE BRAIN CELLS YOU'LL EVER HAVE.

ORIGIN

Picture your brain as the craziest crisscrossed highway system you could ever imagine. Then multiply that network by a million: That gives you an idea of how complicated the human brain is. So the popular opinion among scientists, for a very long time, was that it would be too disruptive for an adult human brain to add a new nerve cell, or neuron, to the mix.

Example. Infinite square well, 3D.

$$-\frac{\hbar^2}{2m}\left(\frac{\partial^2}{\partial x^2} + \frac{\partial^2}{\partial y^2} + \frac{\partial^2}{\partial z^2}\right)\psi_{(x,y,z)} + V\psi = E\psi$$

where $V = 0$ for $\begin{array}{l} 0 < x < a \\ 0 < y < b \\ 0 < z < c \end{array}$

$V = \infty$ otherwise, outside this box, $a \times b \times c$

Inside box, assume a separated solution:

$$\psi_{(x,y,z)} = X(x)\, Y(y)\, Z(z)$$

$$-\frac{\hbar^2}{2m}\left(X''YZ + XY''Z + XYZ''\right) = EXYZ$$

$$-\frac{\hbar^2}{2m}\left(\frac{X''}{X} + \frac{Y''}{Y} + \frac{Z''}{Z}\right) = E$$

all must be constants, separately. k_x^2, k_y^2, k_z^2.

$$X'' = -k_x^2 X \quad \text{etc.} \;\Rightarrow\; X(x) = A\sin(k_x x) \quad A = \sqrt{\frac{2}{a}}$$

$$E = \frac{\hbar^2}{2m}\left(k_x^2 + k_y^2 + k_z^2\right) \quad \text{and} \quad \psi = A\sin(k_x x)\sin(k_y y)\sin(k_z z) \quad A = \sqrt{\frac{2}{a}}\sqrt{\frac{2}{b}}\sqrt{\frac{2}{c}}$$

where $\sin k_x a = 0 \Rightarrow \begin{array}{l} k_x a = l\pi \quad l = 1,2... \\ k_y b = m\pi \quad m = 1,2... \\ k_z c = n\pi \quad n = 1,2... \end{array}$

all bound states:

$$E = \frac{\hbar^2}{2m}\left[\left(\frac{l\pi}{a}\right)^2 + \left(\frac{m\pi}{b}\right)^2 + \left(\frac{n\pi}{c}\right)^2\right] = \frac{\hbar^2 k^2}{2m}$$

and k is like a discrete set of possible values.

$$\langle x \rangle = \int_{-a}^{a} \psi^* \psi\, x\, dx = \int_{-a}^{a} x\,(Ae^{-ax^2})(Ae^{-ax^2})\, dx$$

AS BEFORE

$$\langle x \rangle = A^2\left[\int_{0}^{a} x e^{-2ax^2}\, dx + \int_{-a}^{0} x e^{-2ax^2}\, dx\right]$$

$$\frac{1}{4a}$$

BUT ALSO

$$\int_{x=-\infty}^{0} x e^{-2ax^2} = \int_{x=-\infty}^{0} x e^{-2dx^2}(-dx)$$

$$= -\int_{-\infty}^{0} x e^{-2ax^2} dx$$

$$= -\int_{0}^{\infty} x e^{-2ax^2} dx$$

$$\langle x \rangle = A^2\left[\int_{0}^{\infty} x e^{-2ax^2} dx - \int_{0}^{\infty} x e^{-2ax^2}\right]$$

$$= 0$$

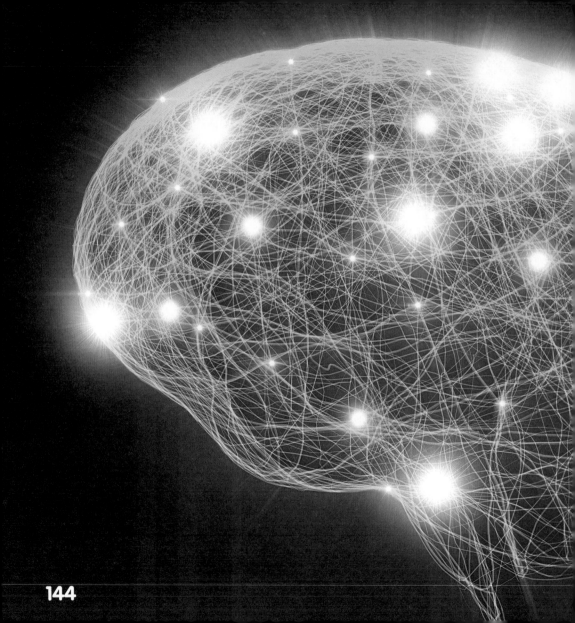

BUSTED!

**IN 1998, A TEAM OF AMERICA
AND SWEDISH SCIENTISTS
REPORTED** that the adult human brain births
neurons in a region called the hippocampus. This seahorse
shaped structure is important for memory and learning. E
studies had shown the birth of neurons in other mature ar
brains, including rats, chickadees, tree shrews, and monk
the last of which—like us—are primates. Scientists are no
investigating the birth of neurons elsewhere in adult mam
brains and how these newbie cells function.

Scientists have discovered some surprisingly
old brains. A 2,500-YEAR-OLD BRAIN was preserved in part by being buried in mud. And
A 4,000-YEAR-OLD BRAIN (that looks like a
burned log) was preserved by being boiled.

MYTH

ANTIBACTERIAL SOAP IS BETTER FOR WASHING YOUR HANDS THAN REGULAR SOAP.

ORIGIN

Both types of soap remove germs by lifting them off the skin and washing them away. But antibacterial soap also contains ingredients that kill germs. That one-two punch may sound better for health. But is it?

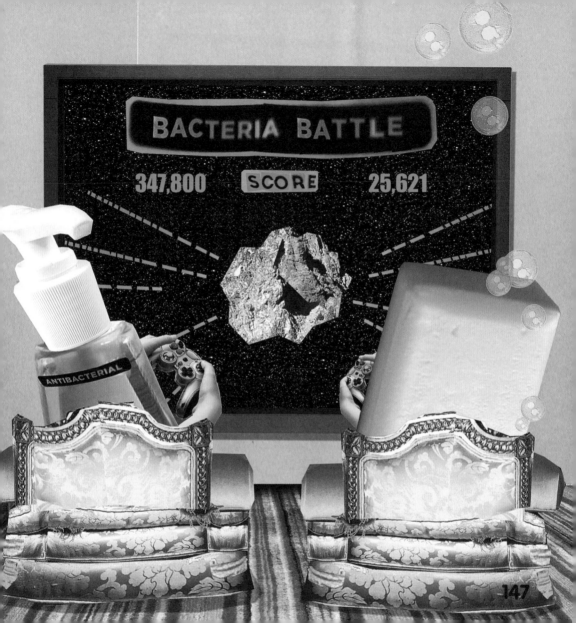

BUSTED!

WHEN IT COMES TO EVERYDAY HANDWASHING IN PLACES LIKE SCHOOL, WORK, AND HOME, antibacterial soap
simply isn't better. In fact, in 2013 the U.S. Food and Drug Administration said this about antibacterial soaps: "There is currently no evidence that they are any more effective at preventing illness than washing with plain soap and water." But that's not the only reason to consider sudsing up with regular soap. Some studies suggest that long-term exposure to antibacterial-soap ingredients may cause health problems in some people and wildlife. And researchers are also looking into whether antibacterial soaps may encourage the most deadly forms of germs to survive.

Scientists recommend washing your hands for AT LEAST 20 SECONDS. To help keep you scrubbing that long, sing the "Happy Birthday" song twice, suggests the U.S. Centers for Disease Control and Prevention.

WHEN TO WASH YOUR HANDS

You don't *constantly* have to wash your hands. But here are ten times when you absolutely should, says the U.S. Centers for Disease Control and Prevention:

1 AFTER TOUCHING AN ANIMAL, ANIMAL FEED, OR ANIMAL WASTE

2 AFTER HANDLING PET FOOD OR PET TREATS

3 BEFORE AND AFTER TREATING A CUT OR WOUND

4 AFTER BLOWING YOUR NOSE, COUGHING, OR SNEEZING

5 BEFORE AND AFTER CARING FOR SOMEONE WHO IS SICK

AFTER CHANGING DIAPERS **6**

AFTER TOUCHING GARBAGE **7**

AFTER USING THE TOILET **8**

9 BEFORE, DURING, AND AFTER PREPARING FOOD

10 BEFORE EATING FOOD

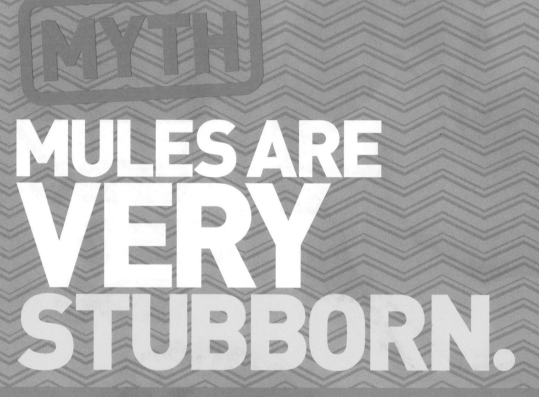

MYTH

MULES ARE VERY STUBBORN.

ORIGIN

A mule is the offspring of a horse and a donkey. You've probably heard the phrase "as stubborn as a mule" (maybe someone has even said this about you!). According to the Oxford English Dictionary, this unfavorable comparison has been around for hundreds of years. Says the dictionary: "With no good grounds, the mule is proverbially regarded as the epitome of obstinacy." What this means: Without good reason, people say mules are the most stubborn of animals. It seems the myth is as stubborn as the mule supposedly is!

BUSTED!

A STUDY PUBLISHED IN 2012 SHOWED THAT MULES AREN'T SO STUBBORN, and in fact, appear to be less stubborn than horses and donkeys. How did scientists determine this? A team of British researchers put mules, donkeys, and horses through a series of problem-solving tests. Among all the animals, mules found solutions the fastest. "Far from being stubborn, they may be more flexible learners than horses and donkeys," say the scientists.

MYTH

SLOTHS SLEEP ALL THE TIME.

ORIGIN

Sloths move slowly, that's for sure. But do they really spend most hours asleep? Studies of both wild and captive sloths have reported that the animals sleep or rest anywhere from 13 to 20 hours a day.

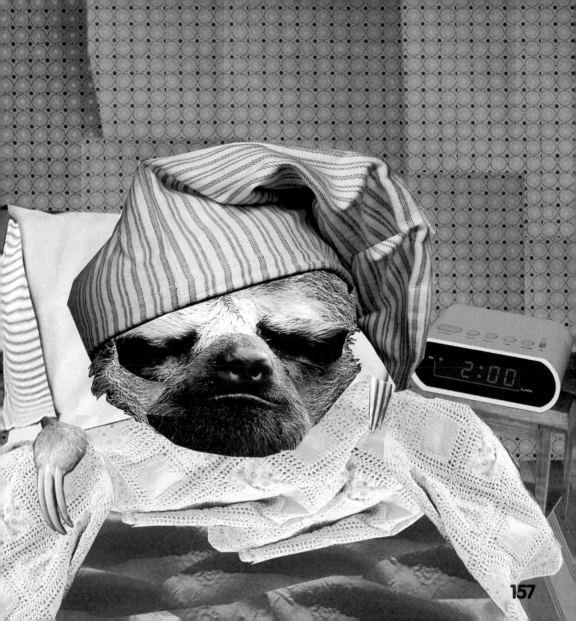

BUSTED!

There's evidence that people may adjust their sleep schedules when living "in captivity," or SPENDING MOST OF THEIR TIME INDOORS. After spending a week camping outdoors in the Rocky Mountains, people WENT TO SLEEP AND WOKE UP ABOUT AN HOUR EARLIER, a University of Colorado Boulder study found.

SLOTH STUDIES PUBLISHED IN 2008 AND 2014 FOUND THAT THE ODD-LOOKING ANIMALS AREN'T SUCH SLEEPYHEADS.

The earlier study was the first to look at the sleep-related brain activity of sloths in the wild; previously, scientists had looked at the brain activity of only captive sloths. For both studies, an international team of scientists caught sloths in Panama and quickly fitted them with miniature devices. These devices recorded the electrical activity in the wearer's brain. By reading the electrical activity patterns, the scientists could tell when the sloths were awake or catching some shut-eye. The teams discovered that sloths in the wild sleep only about 9.6 hours a day—about the same amount the average American teenager requires.

MYTH

BETTY CROCKER WAS A REAL PERSON.

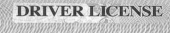

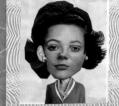

DRIVER LICENSE

BETTY CROCKER
350° Cupcake Crescent
Scrumptious, YUM 12345

Eyes: chocolate
Hair: caramel
Weight: the chef's secret

Betty Crocker

ORIGIN

In 1921, a Minneapolis, Minnesota, U.S.A., flour-milling company began sending responses signed "Betty Crocker" to customers who had mailed in baking questions.

BUSTED!

THE "BETTY CROCKER" SIGNING THOSE LETTERS WASN'T A REAL PERSON.

"Crocker" was the last name of a popular employee who had recently retired, and "Betty" was chosen simply because it sounded friendly. Female employees at the company were asked to submit signatures for "Betty Crocker," and the one chosen is still used by the brand today. An official portrait of Betty Crocker first appeared on a product, a package of cake flour, in 1937. Since then, there have been seven other official portraits of Betty. Her face and hairdo change, but she doesn't seem to age much, and her clothes are always red and white, the brand's colors.

"Betty" cracked the top ten most POPULAR NAMES FOR U.S. BABIES in 1921, the same year Betty Crocker was "born." The name remained in the top ten until 1945.

MYTH

EARTH'S CORE IS MOLTEN, OR LIQUID.

ORIGIN

Over the years, people have said that Earth's mysterious core is (a) hollow, (b) full of dinosaurs, and (c) liquid, to name a few. We've been able to "look" at the planet's deep-down innards for only a little more than a century, with the help of seismographs. These devices don't actually see. Instead, they detect and record seismic waves (those generated by earthquakes and explosions) as they move through Earth. This information helps scientists figure out what the inside of our planet is like.

BUSTED!

You can't DIG A HOLE TO CHINA from the other side of Earth. But in 2012, the deep-sea drilling vessel *Chikyu* dug a hole DEEPER THAN 6,926 FEET (2,111 m) in the sea-floor off Japan. That's more than 1.3 miles (2.1 km) deep!

THE VERY CENTER OF EARTH IS AS SOLID AS A ROCK—

actually, iron and nickel. We know this thanks to a series of seismology studies that discovered our planet's core is not liquid, as had been believed, but rather solid and surrounded by a liquid layer (that's also made of iron and nickel). We now know, too, that the solid inner core is a little smaller than the moon and about as hot as the surface of the sun!

MYTH

FRIDAY THE 13TH IS UNLUCKY.

ORIGIN

Associating Friday the 13th with bad luck goes way back. People have cited 12 months, 12 numbers on the face of a clock, and Jesus Christ's Twelve Apostles, among other things, as evidence that the number 13 is a no-good, leftover oddball. Some buildings don't even have a floor numbered 13, because the superstition around the number is so strong. Combine that with Friday, which superstition in some cultures says is a day of death and other dreadful things, and you've got one *reaaally* bad date: Friday the 13th.

FRIDAY RD

13TH STREET

PARASKEVIDEKATRIAPHOBIA
is the fear of Friday the 13th.

BUSTED!

FRIDAY THE 13TH ISN'T SO BAD.

Researchers have actually investigated whether bad things, like car accidents, happen more often on Friday the 13th. Studies have shown that—yes!—more bad things happen on that date! But then other studies have shown that—no!—bad things don't happen more often on that date. It's up to you to decide whether you want to live in fear on this day, despite a lack of evidence that it really does bring bad luck. But consider this: If you decide to be afraid of this day, will that lessen any of its supposed bad luck? And wouldn't a day lived in fear be a bad day anyway, on its own?

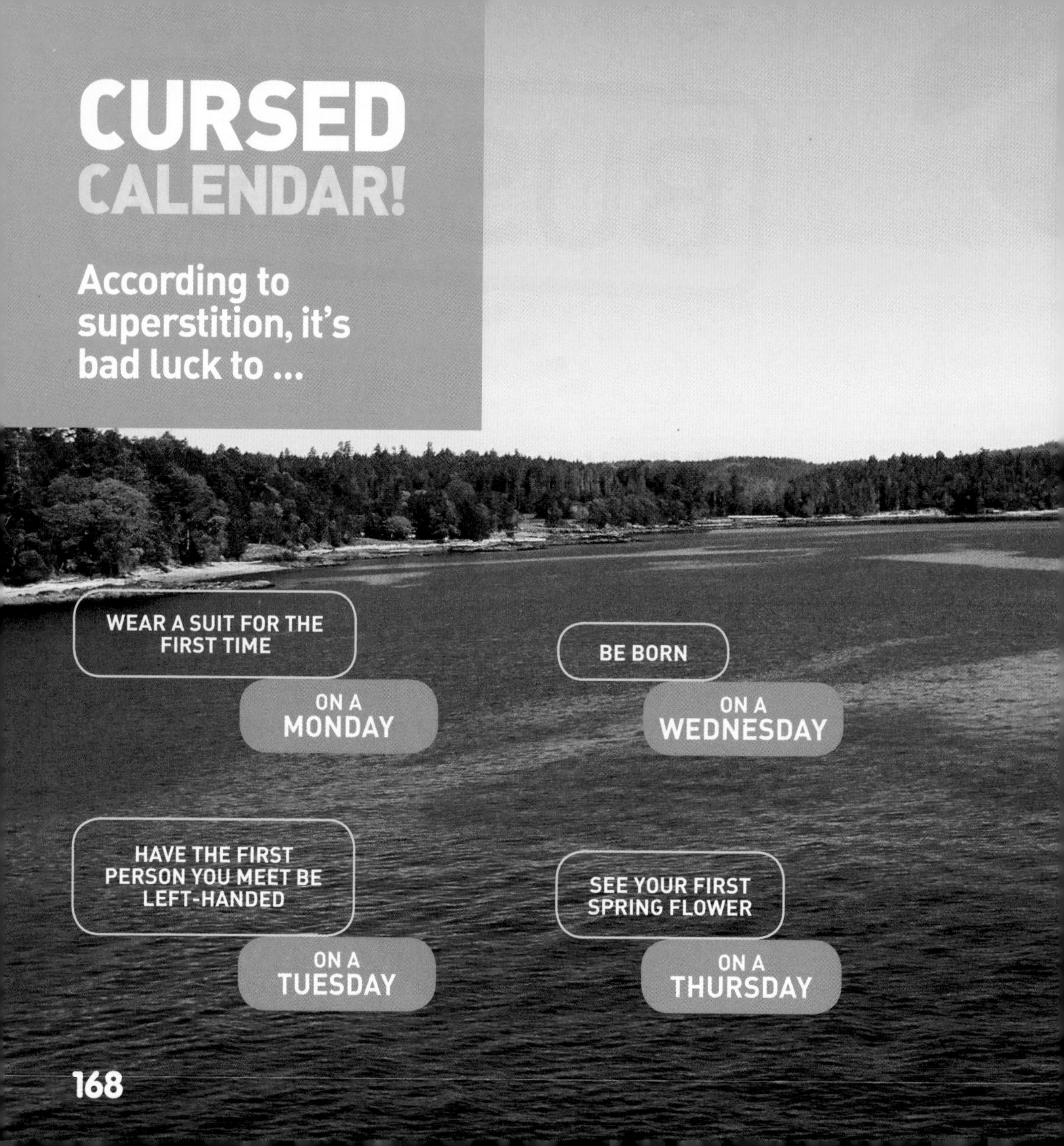

CURSED
CALENDAR!

According to superstition, it's bad luck to ...

WEAR A SUIT FOR THE FIRST TIME

ON A
MONDAY

BE BORN

ON A
WEDNESDAY

HAVE THE FIRST PERSON YOU MEET BE LEFT-HANDED

ON A
TUESDAY

SEE YOUR FIRST SPRING FLOWER

ON A
THURSDAY

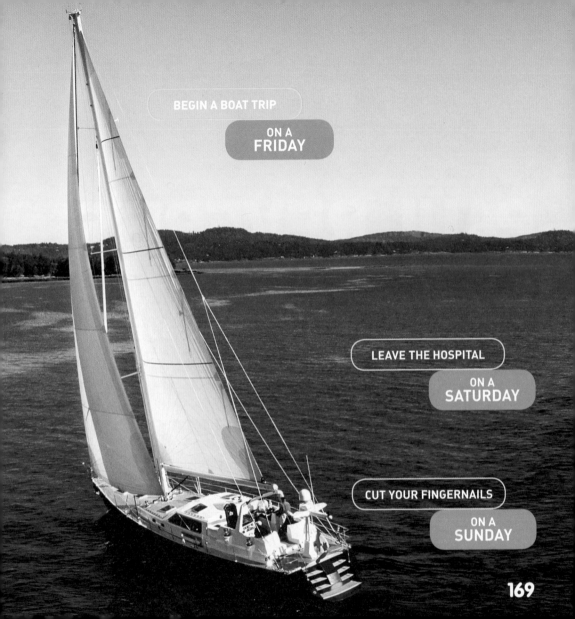

BEGIN A BOAT TRIP
ON A
FRIDAY

LEAVE THE HOSPITAL
ON A
SATURDAY

CUT YOUR FINGERNAILS
ON A
SUNDAY

MYTH

PAUL REVERE'S
HISTORIC RIDE IN 1775
IS ACCURATELY RETOLD IN HENRY
WADSWORTH LONGFELLOW'S 1860 POEM
"PAUL REVERE'S RIDE."

ORIGIN

Many people recall the ride based on a few famous lines from the poem, such as:

Hang a lantern aloft in the belfry arch
Of the North Church tower, as a signal-light,
One, if by land, and two, if by sea;
And I on the opposite shore will be,
Ready to ride and spread the alarm

BUSTED!

LONGFELLOW TWEAKED SOME OF THE DETAILS OF REVERE'S RIDE through Massachusetts, U.S.A., to make it more dramatic. The poet wanted to inspire patriotism among Americans, who were on the verge of the Civil War. Examples of Longfellow's poetic license include the lanterns (they weren't a signal for Revere) and time differences (he arrived in Medford around 11:30 p.m., Lexington around midnight). Perhaps the biggest exaggeration: Revere was the only rider, and he galloped triumphantly into Concord. In fact, after delivering his message that the British were coming, Revere was joined by two other riders: William Dawes and Samuel Prescott. Dawes had also been tasked with delivering the message to Lexington but arrived via a different route. On their way to Concord, all three were arrested by a British patrol. Prescott and Dawes quickly escaped. Revere was released later and never rode on to Concord. Despite these differences in detail, Revere did successfully deliver the message throughout the countryside and is rightfully remembered as an American hero.

News today travels a lot faster than it did during Paul Revere's and Henry Wadsworth Longfellow's times. In the mid-19th century, it took SIX MONTHS FOR A LETTER from Washington, D.C., to arrive in California.

MYTH

THE NORTH STAR IS THE BRIGHTEST STAR IN THE NORTHERN HEMISPHERE'S NIGHTTIME SKY.

ORIGIN

Earth spins around a tilted axis, or an imaginary line that runs through the planet from the North Pole to the South Pole. The star closest to where the northern end of this line points to in space is Polaris. We call it the North Star. For many centuries, people have used Polaris to navigate—find the star, and you've found the direction north. But is this guiding light the brightest of all?

BUSTED!

THE NORTH STAR IS NOT THE BRIGHTEST STAR IN THE NIGHTTIME NORTHERN SKY.

That honor goes to a star named Sirius, which is the brightest star in the southern sky, too. Many more stars are brighter than Polaris, actually. One of them, Vega, will be the North Star about 13,000 years from now. That's because the orientation of Earth's axis shifts slowly over time. While the angle of its tilt remains unchanged, where its axis points to in the sky shifts. As a North Star, Vega will be brighter but it won't be as close to north as Polaris is now, notes Julie Lutz, professor of astronomy at the University of Washington in Seattle. "We're lucky to have a North Star right now that's so effective," she points out.

There is no "South Star" because there's currently NO BRIGHT STAR close to where the southern end of Earth's axis points to in the sky.

MORE
STELLAR
STARS

BIGGEST AND BRIGHTEST
PISTOL
(about 100 times as massive as the sun, and 10,000,000 times brighter!)

OLDEST
HD 140283
(nicknamed "Methuselah"; at least 13.8 billion years old!)

MOST FUN NAME TO SAY
BETELGEUSE
(pronounced BAY-tell-juice)

CLOSEST TO EARTH
THE SUN
93,000,000 miles
(149,600,000 km)

SECOND CLOSEST TO EARTH
PROXIMA CENTAURI
24,793,000,000,000 miles
(39,900,000,000,000 km)!

THERE'S A DINOSAUR NAMED *BRONTOSAURUS.*

ORIGIN

In the late 1800s, two sets of unearthed dinosaur fossils caused a colossal mix-up. The first set of fossils found was named *Apatosaurus;* the second, later set was named *Brontosaurus.*

IT TURNS OUT THE TWO SETS OF FOSSILS WERE REALLY THE SAME TYPE OF DINOSAUR.

The mistake was discovered in the early 1900s, and the single species took the first name given to it, *Apatosaurus*. But by then, the name *Brontosaurus* had become more popular, and the now incorrect name for the species stuck. Further confusing things, the wrong skulls—they belonged to *Camarasaurus*—were placed atop *Apatosaurus* skeletons in several American museums. It took until the 1990s to put all the correct skulls in place.

BUSTED!

Though *Apatosaurus* was a beast—topping out at 90 FEET (27 M) LONG— it was a plant-eater.

MYTH

ALBERT EINSTEIN, RENOWNED MATH AND PHYSICS GENIUS, FAILED MATH AS A KID.

ORIGIN

Many people think that a 1935 newspaper column first made the hard-to-believe claim that Einstein, winner of the 1921 Nobel Prize in physics, flunked math as a kid.

A CHALKBOARD with an equation written on it by Albert Einstein during a 1931 lecture is housed at the MUSEUM OF THE HISTORY OF SCIENCE in Oxford, England. It's one of the museum's most popular items.

ALBERT EINSTEIN NEVER FAILED MATH

class, says Diana Kormos-Buchwald, editor of *The Collected Papers of Albert Einstein* and professor of history at the California Institute of Technology. She should know: She's seen his grades. She assumes the myth stems from confusion over which number was best in the grading system—a scale of 1 to 6—in Switzerland, where Einstein attended high school and university. In fact, she says, "he was an excellent student from age 5 to 25, and he jumped ahead and was the youngest student in his grade all through university."

MYTH

SUMMER HAPPENS
WHEN EARTH'S ORBIT BRINGS US
CLOSEST TO THE SUN.

WINTER HAPPENS
WHEN THE PLANET'S ORBIT TAKES US
FARTHEST FROM THE SUN.

ORIGIN

Our planet orbits the sun in an imperfect circular path. A lot of people assume that summer's abundant daylight and hotter temperatures are because Earth's orbit has brought it closest to the sun. And, the thinking goes, when Earth and the sun are farthest from each other, the planet experiences the darker, colder days of winter.

BUSTED!

SEASONS DON'T HAPPEN AT THE SAME TIME ALL OVER THE WORLD.

If it's summer in the Northern Hemisphere, it's winter in the Southern Hemisphere, and vice versa. So, the planet can't be both its closest and farthest distance from the sun at the same time. The reason for the seasons is the planet's tilt: Earth leans at a 23.5-degree angle. It spins, while tilted, as it orbits the sun. The half of the world experiencing summer does so because that part of the planet is at that time tilted toward the sun. At the same time, the other half of the world experiences winter because it's tilted away from the sun. It turns out that in January—winter in the Northern Hemisphere, summer in the Southern Hemisphere—Earth passes closest to the sun. In July—summer in the Northern Hemisphere, winter in the Southern Hemisphere—Earth is at its farthest distance from the sun.

Aphelion is the point at which Earth's orbit takes it FARTHEST FROM THE SUN. Perihelion is when the planet is CLOSEST TO THE SUN. The difference in aphelion and perihelion distances is only a few million miles (km).

"FAINTING GOATS" PASS OUT WHEN STARTLED.

ORIGIN

These domestic goats are known for their sudden, awkward falls. Reports of them first surfaced in Tennessee, U.S.A., in the late 1800s. The animals, which are very muscular, are raised for meat and kept as pets.

BUSTED!

WHEN FAINTING GOATS FALL OVER, IT'S NOT BECAUSE THEY'VE PASSED OUT.

The real reason is even weirder. Because of a genetic quirk, the goats' muscles lock up for a prolonged period of time when the animals are startled or step over low barriers. Stiff-legged, the goats topple over. But don't worry: They're down for the count for only a few moments.

It's estimated there are only about 10,000 FAINTING GOATS in the world.

MYTH

A RABBIT'S DIET CONSISTS MOSTLY OF CARROTS.

ORIGIN

The idea that rabbits live on carrots is usually traced back to the cartoon character Bugs Bunny, who first appeared in movies 75 years ago. He became famous for chomping on carrots and delivering the line: "Eh, what's up, doc?"

MENU

APPETIZERS

Carrots
Carrot Soup
Carrot Salad

MENU

ENTRÉES

Fillet of Carrots

Carrot Ragout

Roasted Carrots
on a Bed of Carrots

Desserts

Flaming Carrot

Carrot Pudding

Carrot Cake

BUST

WILD RABBITS DON'T RELY ON CARROTS AS THEIR MAIN MEAL.

And if pet rabbits are fed mostly or only carrots, "several problems will crop up," says Seattle veterinarian Dan Lejnieks. "Fresh, dried hay with limited greens, fruits, and vegetables is what we recommend, and pellets are optional." Fruits and starchy vegetables like carrots should be treated as desserts, given in very small amounts. Too many carrots would cause digestive problems, including excess gas. And chomping on carrots all day wouldn't wear down rabbit teeth, which constantly grow, in the right way. "Hay wears teeth properly because it's so coarse," explains Lejnieks.

The Bunnicula children's book series stars a "VAMPIRE" RABBIT that sucks the juices from vegetables.

MYTH

SNAKES HYPNOTIZE, OR CHARM, THEIR PREY.

ORIGIN

"Look into my eyessssssss." For centuries, people have said snakes have special powers, including the ability to hypnotize their prey. Perhaps it's a snake's unblinking eyes. Or the way a snake sways its head while eyeing its prey, which sometimes freezes instead of fleeing.

BUSTED!

THERE'S NO EVIDENCE THAT SNAKES PUT THEIR PREY IN A TRANCELIKE STATE before pouncing on them. Instead, scientists say, it's likely that prey stay put out of fear, curiosity, or in the hopes that the snakes won't detect them. As for those unblinking eyes: You wouldn't blink, either, if you didn't have eyelids. And that head swaying: It might help snakes better keep track of their target.

According to legend, snakes themselves can be hypnotized by PEAFOWL.

MORE SNAKE MYTHS BUSTED

SOME SNAKES CAN STICK THEIR TAIL IN THEIR MOUTH AND ROLL AWAY.

As cool as it sounds, snakes can't contort their bodies into a circle and roll away.

SNAKES STING AND WHIP.

Snakes bite, spit, and squeeze, not sting and whip.

MILKSNAKES SNEAK INTO BARNS TO DRINK THE MILK FROM COWS.

Though frequently found on farms, these snakes don't slurp milk from animals— no snake does! Milksnakes instead often enter barns in search of rodents and other tasty morsels to eat.

SNAKES ARE EVIL.

Snakes aren't out to get you, and only about one in ten are venomous.

SNAKES ARE SLIMY.

Snakes are scaly, not slimy, and dry, quite often smooth.

INDEX

Illustrations are indicated by **boldface.**

INDEX

For Moo —EK

STAFF FOR THIS BOOK
Becky Baines, *Senior Editor*
Callie Broaddus, *Art Director and Designer*
Hillary Leo, *Photo Editor*
Paige Towler, *Editorial Assistant*
Sanjida Rashid, *Design Production Assistant*
Michael Cassady, *Photo Assistant*
Grace Hill, *Associate Managing Editor*
Mike O'Connor, *Production Editor*
Lewis R. Bassford, *Production Manager*
Rachel Faulise, *Manager, Production Services*
Susan Borke, *Legal and Business Affairs*

PUBLISHED BY THE NATIONAL GEOGRAPHIC SOCIETY
Gary E. Knell, *President and CEO*
John M. Fahey, *Chairman of the Board*
Melina Gerosa Bellows, *Chief Education Officer*
Declan Moore, *Chief Media Officer*
Hector Sierra, *Senior Vice President and General Manager
 Book Division*

**SENIOR MANAGEMENT TEAM, KIDS PUBLISHING
AND MEDIA**
Nancy Laties Feresten, *Senior Vice President;* Jennifer Emmett, *Vice President, Editorial Director, Kids Books;* Julie Vosburgh Agnone, *Vice President, Editorial Operations;* Rachel Buchholz, *Editor and Vice President,* NG Kids *magazine;* Michelle Sullivan, *Vice President, Kids Digital;* Eva Absher-Schantz, *Design Director;* Jay Sumner, *Photo Director;* Hannah August, *Marketing Director;* R. Gary Colbert, *Production Director*

DIGITAL
Anne McCormack, *Director;* Laura Goertzel, Sara Zeglin, *Producers;* Jed Winer, *Special Projects Assistant;* Emma Rigney, *Creative Producer;* Brian Ford, *Video Producer;* Bianca Bowman, *Assistant Producer;* Natalie Jones, *Senior Product Manager*

For more information, please visit nationalgeographic.com, call 1-800-NGS LINE (647-5463), or write to the following address:
National Geographic Society
1145 17th Street N.W.
Washington, D.C. 20036-4688 U.S.A.

Visit us online at nationalgeographic.com/books

For librarians and teachers: ngchildrensbooks.org

More for kids from National Geographic:
kids.nationalgeographic.com

For information about special discounts for bulk purchases, please contact National Geographic Books Special Sales: ngspecsales@ngs.org

For rights or permissions inquiries, please contact National Geographic Books Subsidiary Rights: ngbookrights@ngs.org

Library of Congress Cataloging-in-Publication Data

Krieger, Emily.
 Myths busted! 3 : just when you thought you knew what you knew / Emily Krieger.
    pages cm. -- (Myths busted)
 Includes index.
  ISBN 978-1-4263-1883-2 (pbk.) -- ISBN 978-1-4263-1884-9 (reinforced library binding)
 1. Common fallacies--Juvenile literature. I. Title. II. Title: Myths busted: Three.
 AZ999.K753 2015
 001.9'6--dc23
                                                    2014036193

Printed in Hong Kong
15/THK/1

ABOUT THE ART

"To make these crazy collages, I start with a line drawing and layer pieces of collage on top. Backgrounds can start as torn paper doodles and then become landscapes or interiors. It's amazing what you can make from a scrap of paper!"

—Tom Nick Cocotos

Check out the artist online! www.cocotos.com

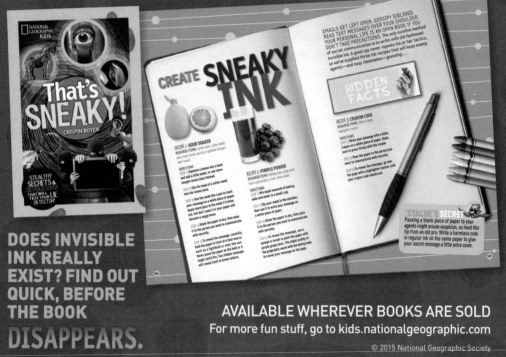